Words
OF
Comfort

ANDREWS AND McMEEL
A UNIVERSAL PRESS SYNDICATE COMPANY
KANSAS CITY

ISBN: 0-8362-1072-7

Printed in Singapore
First U.S. edition

1   3   5   7   9   10   8   6   4   2

Edited by Linda Sunshine
Designed by Susi Oberhelman
Produced by Smallwood and Stewart, Inc.
New York City

Notice: Every effort has been made to locate the copyright owners of the
material used in the book. Please let us know if an error has been made, and we
will make any necessary changes in subsequent printings.

Credits and copyright notices appear on page 70.

INTRODUCTION

"*All in the end is harvest.*"
—EDITH SITWELL

As the old saying goes, there is much to be learned through loss and great wisdom to be gained through suffering. "We will grieve not, rather find/Strength in what remains behind" wrote Wordsworth, who always seemed to have the best things to say when words are hard to come by.

Ultimately, what truly consoles us through the hardships of life is the presence of grace and the immortality of love. From adversity we discover these twin mercies—love and grace—but the lessons are not easily learned.

I thought I knew something about loss. I'd had boyfriends who left and pets that died. But I was thirty-four years old before I realized there was much I had yet to learn.

That was the year my father died and everything changed. I was like a tightrope walker who looks down and discovers her safety net has vanished. I felt an emptiness so profound it was as though I had a big black hole where my heart used to be. It took me a long time, and a lot of help and support, to realize how much my dad meant to me, how he had shaped my life, and how much I truly loved him. Only a strange thing happened when I acknowledged my loss: I got my father back.

He comes to me now in dreams so real that I wake up smiling, feeling as though we've just visited. I think of him often and of the many things he taught me, not so much by what he said, but by who he was. His gifts—his love of words, his dignity, his sense of justice—have become my guideposts.

I discovered that you never really lose someone you love, they are with you always, just as my dad is with me in my dreams, in my work, in my life, and this knowledge is a wellspring of comfort and peace. "When one door of happiness closes, another opens," wrote Helen Keller.

Other writers have eloquently written about their own triumphs over hardships and the strength to be found on the other side of that closed door. Read the words of Annie Dillard, William Styron, Wallace Stegner, and Anne Tyler, among many others, and know that none of us is alone. There is great solace to be found here among these writers who share their sorrows, and perhaps more importantly, describe the cyclical nature of their triumphs and spirituality. For it is these very cycles of life with which we are all blessed and cursed, confused and consoled, and, in the end, molded into becoming the people we are today. I am, and always will be, my father's daughter.

—LINDA SUNSHINE

Words seem very poor things at such a time of trouble as yours and yet they are all one can use to tell of one's sympathy.

MAISIE WARD
Father Maturin

GRIEF REMAINS ONE OF THE FEW THINGS THAT HAS THE POWER TO SILENCE US. IT IS A WHISPER IN THE WORLD AND A CLAMOR WITHIN. MORE THAN SEX, MORE THAN FAITH, EVEN MORE THAN ITS USHER DEATH, GRIEF IS UNSPOKEN, PUBLICLY IGNORED EXCEPT FOR THOSE MOMENTS AT THE FUNERAL THAT ARE OVER TOO QUICKLY, OR THE CONVERSATIONS AMONG THE COGNOSCENTI, THOSE OF US WHO RECOGNIZE IN ONE ANOTHER A KINDRED CHASM DEEP IN THE CENTER OF WHO WE ARE.

MAYBE WE DO NOT SPEAK OF IT

BECAUSE DEATH WILL MARK ALL OF US, SOONER OR

LATER. OR MAYBE IT IS UNSPOKEN BECAUSE GRIEF IS

ONLY THE FIRST PART OF IT. AFTER A TIME IT BECOMES

SOMETHING LESS SHARP BUT LARGER, TOO, A MORE

ENDURING THING CALLED LOSS.

PERHAPS THAT IS WHY THIS IS

THE LEAST EXPLORED PASSAGE: BECAUSE IT HAS NO

END. THE WORLD LOVES CLOSURE, LOVES A THING

THAT CAN, AS THEY SAY, BE GOTTEN THROUGH. THIS

IS WHY IT COMES AS A GREAT SURPRISE TO FIND

THAT LOSS IS FOREVER, THAT TWO DECADES AFTER

THE EVENT THERE ARE THOSE OCCASIONS WHEN

SOMETHING IN YOU CRIES OUT AT THE CONTINUOUS

PRESENCE OF AN ABSENCE. "AN AWFUL LEISURE,"

EMILY DICKINSON ONCE CALLED WHAT THE LIVING

HAVE AFTER DEATH. . . .

THE LANDSCAPES OF ALL OUR LIVES

BECOME AS FULL OF CRATERS AS THE SURFACE

OF THE MOON. MY BROTHER IS A YOUNG WIDOWER

WITH YOUNG CHILDREN, AS HIS FATHER WAS

BEFORE HIM. AND I WRITE MY OBITUARIES CARE-

FULLY AND THINK ABOUT HOW LITTLE THE FACTS

SUFFICE, NOT ONLY TO DESCRIBE THE DEAD BUT

TO TELL WHAT THEY WILL MEAN TO THE LIVING

ALL THE REST OF OUR LIVES. WE ARE DEFINED BY

WHOM WE HAVE LOST.

ANNA QUINDLEN
Life After Death

NIGHT

brings out stars as

SORROWS

show us truths.

PHILIP JAMES BAILEY, *Truth and Sorrows*

So I lost myself in the oils and

After her funeral, a sadness took over me that seemed permanent, and I lost myself in the details and technicalities connected to death in the South. Great sorrow still needs to be fed and I dealt with my disconsolate emptiness by feeding everyone who gathered around me to offer their support. I felt as though I were providing sustenance for the entire army in the field who had come together to ease the malignant ache I felt every time Shyla's name was mentioned. The word Shyla itself became a land mine. That sweet-sounding word was merciless and I could not bear to hear it.

condiments of my well-stocked kitc

I fatted up my friends and family, attempted complicated recipes I had always put off making, and even tried my hand at Asian cuisine for the first time. With six gas burners ablaze, I turned out velvety soups and rib-sticking stews. I alternated between cooking and weeping and I prayed for the repose of the soul of my sad, hurt wife. I suffered, I grieved, I broke down, and I cooked fabulous meals for those who came to comfort me.

PAT CONROY
Beach Music

We pull ourselves together when we need to. We do the things that have to be done. But we need to give ourselves times and places in which to mourn. This is strength, not weakness.

MADELEINE L'ENGLE
Two-Part Invention

ow, when Hubert died, that really hurt. He was just shy of ninety years old. It never made a bit of difference to me that Hubert became an assistant United States attorney, a judge, and all that. He was still my little brother.

Same way with Hap. You know what? Even when he was ninety-five years old, Sadie and I still spoiled him. When he didn't like what they were cooking for dinner at his house, he would get up and leave the table and come over here and we'd fix him what he liked to eat.

Good ol' Hap knew he was going to Glory and he was content. He said, "I've had a good life. I've done everything I wanted to do, I think I've done right by people." We Delanys can usually say that, when our time comes.

SARAH AND A. ELIZABETH DELANY
WITH AMY HILL HEARTH
Having Our Say

Hope the voyage

is a long one.

May there be many a summer morning when,
with what pleasure, what joy,
you come into harbors seen for the first time;
may you stop at Phoenician trading stations
to buy fine things,
mother of pearl and coral, amber and ebony,
sensual perfume of every kind—
as many sensual perfumes as you can,
and may you visit many Egyptian cities
to gather stores of knowledge from their scholars.

Keep Ithakacq always in your mind.
Arriving there is what you are destined for.
But do not hurry the journey at all.

C. P. CAVAFY
Ithaka

THANK HEAVEN FOR

what happiness you have,
and after thinking a
moment or two that you
suffer in common with
all mankind hold it
not a sin to regain your
cheerfulness.

JOHN KEATS

am living on a planet where the silk dresses of Renaissance women rustled, where people died in plagues, where Mozart sat to play, where sap runs in the spring, where children are caught in crossfire, where gold glints from rock, where religion shines its light only to lose its way, where people stop to reach a hand to help each other cross, where much is known about the life of the ant, where the gift of getting my husband back was as accidental as my almost losing him, where the star called sun shows itself differently at every hour, where people get so bruised and confused they kill each other, where baobabs grow into impossible shapes with trunks that tell stories to hands, where rivers wind wide and green with terrible hidden currents, where you rise in the morning and feel your own arms with your own hands, checking yourself, where lovers' hearts swell with the certain knowledge that only they are the ones, where viruses are seen under the insistent eye of the microscope and the birth of stars is witnessed through the lens of the telescope, where caterpillars crawl and skyscrapers are erected because of the blue line on the blueprint—I am living here on this planet, it is my time to have my legs walk the earth, and I am turning around to tell Jay once again, "Yes, here." I am saying that all of this, all of this, all of these things are the telling songs of the wider life, and I am listening with gratitude, and I am listening for as long as I can, and I am listening with all of my might.

ELIZABETH BERG, *Range of Motion*

When one door of happiness

closes, another opens; but often

we look so long at the closed

door that we do not see the one

which has been opened for us.

HELEN KELLER

or those who have dwelt in depression's dark wood, and known its inexplicable agony, their return from the abyss is not unlike the ascent of the poet, trudging upward and upward out of hell's black depths and at last emerging into what he saw as "the shining world." There, whoever has been restored to health has almost always been restored to the capacity for serenity and joy, and this may be indemnity enough for having endured the despair beyond despair.

E quindi uscimmo a riveder le stelle.

And so we came forth, and once again beheld the stars.

WILLIAM STYRON
Darkness Visible

e are hardly lost in the universe. To the contrary, the reality of grace indicates humanity to be at the center of the universe. This time and space exists for us to travel through. When my patients lose sight of their significance and are disheartened by the effort of the work we are doing, I sometimes tell them that the human race is in the midst of making an evolutionary leap. "Whether or not we succeed in that leap," I say to them, "is your personal responsibility." And mine. The universe, this stepping-stone, has been laid down to prepare a way for us. But we ourselves must step across it, one by one. Through grace we are helped not to stumble and through grace we know that we are being welcomed. What more can we ask?

M. SCOTT PECK
The Road Less Traveled

NATURE OFTEN OFFERS METAPHORS MORE ELEGANT
than any we can manufacture,
and Muir Woods is no exception.
Redwoods have evolved to turn

disaster into opportunity. In these coastal forests, death produces life.

This is what I mean: In the redwood ecosystem, buds for future trees are contained in pods called burls, tough brown knobs that cling to the bark of the mother tree. When the mother tree is logged, blown over, or destroyed by fire— when, in other words, she dies—the trauma stimulates the burls' growth hormones. The seeds release, and trees sprout around her, creating the circle of daughters. The daughter trees grow by absorbing the sunlight their mother cedes to them when she dies. And they get the moisture and nutrients they need from their mother's root system, which remains intact underground even after her leaves die. Although the daughters exist independently of their mother above ground, they continue to draw sustenance from her underneath.

I am fooling only myself when I say my mother exists now only in the photograph on my bulletin board or in the outline of my hand or in the armful of memories I still hold tight. She lives on beneath everything I do. Her presence influenced who I was, and her absence influences who I am. Our lives are shaped as much by those who leave us as they are by those who stay. Loss is our legacy. Insight is our gift. Memory is our guide.

HOPE EDELMAN
Motherless Daughters

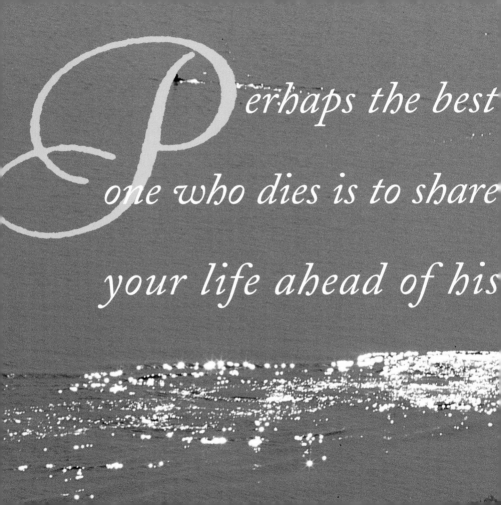

Perhaps the best one who dies is to share your life ahead of his

ribute you can pay some

his belief in life by putting

death.

MAX LERNER, *The Unfinished Country*

It is

often said that something may survive of a person after his death, if that person was an artist and put a little of himself into his work. It is perhaps in the same way that a sort of cutting taken from one person and grafted onto the heart of another continues to carry on its existence even when the person from whom it had been detached has perished.

MARCEL PROUST
Remembrance of Things Past

esolately I went back to raking litter out from under the yellow hedge. New growth caught in the teeth, and when I bent to look I saw that it was poison oak. Though I had sprayed every resurgent clump and bush for two years and more, and had cleaned the hill, now some bird or wind had dropped a berry and started me a new crop where it would be the devil itself to spray without killing what I wanted to preserve.

You wondered what was in whale's milk. Now you know. Think of the force down there, just telling things to get born, just to be!

I had had no answer for her then. Now I might have one. Yes, think of it, I might say. And think of how random and indiscriminate it is, think how helplessly we must submit, think how impossible it is to control or direct it. Think how often beauty and delicacy and grace are choked out by weeds. Think how endless and dubious is the progress from weed to flower.

Even alive, she never convinced me with her advocacy of biological perfectionism. She never persuaded me to ignore, or to look upon as merely hard pleasures, the evil that I felt in every blight and smut and pest in my garden—that I felt, for that matter, squatting like a toad on my own heart. Think of the force of life, yes, but think of the component of darkness in it. One of the things that's in whale's milk is the promise of pain and death.

And so? Admitting what is so obvious, what then? Would I wipe Marian Catlin out of my unperfected consciousness if I could? Would I forgo the pleasure of her company to escape the bleakness of her loss? Would I go back to my own formula, which was twilight sleep, to evade the pain she brought with her?

Not for a moment. And so even in the gnashing of my teeth I acknowledge my conversion. It turns out to be for me as I once told her it would be for her daughter. I shall be richer all my life for this sorrow.

WALLACE STEGNER
All the Little Live Things

There is an overall plan of
which you are not aware
and to which you can only
contribute by being who
you are, doing your best,
seeking your higher truth,
and following your heart.

PAT RODEGAST AND JUDITH STANTON
Emmanuel's Book

DIVINITY IS NOT PLAYFUL.
The universe was not made in jest but in
solemn incomprehensible earnest. By a power
that is unfathomably secret, and holy, and
fleet. There is nothing to be done about it,
but ignore it, or see. And then you walk
fearlessly, eating what you must, growing

wherever you can, like the monk on the road

who knows precisely how vulnerable he is,

who takes no comfort among death-forgetting

men, and who carries his vision of vastness

and might around in his tunic like a live coal

which neither burns nor warms him, but

with which he will not part.

ANNIE DILLARD, *Pilgrim at Tinker Creek*

Death is no more a defeat
than is growing taller, starting
school, or falling in love.
All are phases of life, and
each brings with it a special
set of hazards and satisfactions.
To live with grace we must
be prepared to die with grace.

ARNOLD R. BEISSER
A Graceful Passage

I see an empty place at the table.

Whose? Who else's? Who am I kidding?

The boat's waiting. No need for oars

or a wind. I've left the key

in the same place. You know where.

Remember me and all we did together.

Now, hold me tight. That's it. Kiss me

hard on the lips. There. Now

let me go, my dearest. Let me go.

We shall not meet again in this life,

So kiss me goodbye now. Here, kiss me again.

Once more. There. That's enough.

Now, my dearest, let me go.

It's time to be on the way.

RAYMOND CARVER
No Need

Without dreams and ph

LONG YEARS BEFORE the father had walked in the little cabin, and seen choirs of angels, and a prince like unto men, but clothed in immortality. The son's knowledge was not as the father's, therefore the dream was new-tinted, but the sweetness was all there, the infinite peace, that men find not in the little cankered kingdom of the tangible. The bars of the real are set close about us; we cannot open our wings but they are struck against them, and drop bleeding. But, when we glide between the bars into the great unknown beyond, we may sail forever in the glorious blue, seeing nothing but our own shadows.

So age succeeds age, and dream succeeds dream, and of the joy of the dreamer no man knoweth but he who dreameth.

Our fathers had their dreams; we have ours; the generation that follows will have its own.

toms man cannot exist.

OLIVE SCHEINER
The Story of an African Farm

"Look at the

clouds

"They pass so gently and so quietly,

but as if with such resolution.

Someone once said they were rafts for t

essandro said.

souls."

MARK HELPRIN, *A Soldier of the Great War*

was wondering if you thought of her often now that you're back in the house where she used to be. I think of her often too. She may not be here herself anymore, but the memory's here, isn't it, and

memories are so precious

because no one can take them away from you, and although she's dead yet in a way she's still alive, alive in your mind, and that's how God can bring her back for you. And although that's not as good as having her here alive and well, it helps to look across at the past, doesn't it, to look at her and know that she'll be there always in your memory to be a comfort to you when you want to remember.

SUSAN HOWATCH
Wheel of Fortune

such a comfort,

We give them back to you, dear Lord,
who gavest them to us.
Yet as thou didst not lose them in giving,
so we have not lost them by their return.
For what is thine is ours always
    if we are thine.
And life is eternal and love is immortal,
and death is only a horizon,
and a horizon is nothing more
than the limit of our sight.

Quaker Prayer

THEY PASSED THE BOY once again. He had a jaunty, stiff-legged way of walking that seemed familiar.

If Ethan hadn't died, Macon thought, wouldn't he have grown into such a person? . . .

And if dead people aged, wouldn't it be a comfort? To think of Ethan growing up in heaven—fourteen years old now instead of twelve—eased the grief a little. Oh, it was their immunity to time that made the dead so heartbreaking. (Look at the husband who dies young, the wife aging on without him; how sad to imagine the husband coming back to find her so changed.) Macon gazed out the cab window, considering the notion in his mind. He felt a kind of inner rush, a racing forward. The real adventure, he thought, is the flow of time; it's as much adventure as anyone could wish. And if he pictured Ethan still part of that flow—in some other place however unreachable—he believed he might be able to bear it after all.

ANNE TYLER
Accidental Tourist

ankind, for all its unique gifts, is just as much a part of the ecosystem as is any other zoologic or botanical form, and nature does not distinguish. We die so that the world may continue to live. We have been given the miracle of life because trillions upon trillions of living things have prepared the way for us and then have died—in a sense, for us. We die, in turn, so that others may live. The tragedy of a single individual becomes, in the balance of natural things, the triumph of ongoing life.

All of this makes more precious each hour of those we have been given; it demands that life must be useful and rewarding. If by our work and pleasure, our triumphs and our failures, each of us is contributing to an evolving process of continuity not only of our species but of the entire balance of nature, the dignity we create in the time allotted to us becomes a continuum with the dignity we achieve by the altruism of accepting the necessity of death.

SHERWIN B. NULAND
How We Die

WE WALKED, THAT WINTER EVENING, IN THE FIELDS together; and the blessed calm within us seemed to be partaken by the frosty air. The early stars began to shine while we were lingering on, and looking up to them, we thanked God for having guided us to this tranquillity.

WE STOOD TOGETHER IN THE SAME OLD-FASHIONED window at night, when the moon was shining; Agnes with her quiet eyes raised up to it; I following her glance. Long miles of road then opened out before my mind; and, toiling on, I saw a ragged way-worn boy forsaken and neglected, who should come to call even the heart now beating against mine, his own.

CHARLES DICKENS
David Copperfield

WE COME NOW TO THE END OF THESE

THE WATERS OF OUR MIND, THE

AND ARE GONE AS INSTANTLY ~ LIKE WHISPERS. HOW IS IT WE HAVE NOTHIN

A FRAGILE HOPE, THE KNOWLEDGE OF OUR UNIT, AN

ALL BECAUSE THESE LETTERS, BECKONING U

ACCOUNTS, THE FALLEN LEAVES DRIFTING ON

NGELS' LETTERS THAT HAVE COME ~

ERE THEY REALLY THERE?

OW TO SHOW FOR THEM EXCEPT A SENSE OF GRACE,

SWEET SHIVER PASSING OVER US,

O HIGHER STATES, CARRY THE SIGNATURE OF GOD?

SOPHY BURNHAM, *Angel Letters*

ACKNOWLEDGMENTS

From "Private & Public; Life After Death," by Anna Quindlen, 5/4/94. Copyright © 1994 by The New York Times Company. Reprinted by permission.

From *Beach Music* by Pat Conroy. Copyright © 1995 by Pat Conroy. Used by permission of Doubleday, a division of Bantam Doubleday Dell Publishing Group, Inc.

From *Two-Part Invention: The Story of a Marriage* by Madeleine L'Engle. Copyright © 1988 by Crosswicks Limited. Reprinted by permission of Farrar, Straus & Giroux Inc.

From *Having Our Say: The Delany Sisters' First 100 Years* by Sarah and Elizabeth Delany with Amy Hill Hearth, copyright © 1993 by Amy Hill Hearth, Sarah Louise Delany and Annie Elizabeth Delany, reprinted by permission of Kodansha America, Inc.

Cavafy, C. P.; *Ithaka*. Copyright © 1992 rev. edn. by Keeley/Sherrard Trans. Reprinted by permission of Princeton University Press.

Berg, Elizabeth, *Range of Motion*, copyright © 1995 by Elizabeth Berg, reprinted by permission of Random House Inc.

Styron, William, *Darkness Visible*, copyright © 1990 by William Styron, reprinted by permission of Alfred A. Knopf/Random House.

Reprinted with the permission of Simon & Schuster from *The Road Less Traveled* by M. Scott Peck, M.D. Copyright © 1978 by M. Scott Peck, M.D.

Hope Edelman, *Motherless Daughters*, © 1994 by Hope Edelman. Reprinted by permission of Addison-Wesley Publishing Company, Inc.

Excerpt from *All the Little Live Things* by Wallace Stegner. Copyright © 1967 by Wallace Stegner (Penguin, USA). All rights reserved. Reprinted by permission of Brandt and Brandt Literary Agents, Inc.

From *Emmanuel's Book* by Pat Rodegast & Judith Stanton. Copyright © 1985 by Pat Rodegast. Used by permission of